This book belongs to

_____

This book is dedicated to my supportive husband Quentin and my inspiring little doers, Zoe and Caleb.

I May Be Little
But I Can Do A Lot

Written By Ama Darkwa Holmes

Illustrated by Jeanne Ee

My name is Zoe and I'm 6 years old.

"You'll change the world little one!"
is what I have been told.

So I started to believe it,
now it's my favorite thought,

I may

be little

*but I can
do a lot!*

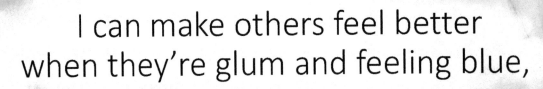

I can make others feel better
when they're glum and feeling blue,

with a hug and a smile,
I'll always be there for you.

I can learn new things
like a language or a sport,

with my brain and lots of practice
I will never fall short.

I can have a positive attitude
in everything I do,

with my best effort and discipline,
I'll always prevail too.

I can try different ways
and learn from my mistakes,

with persistence and grit
in every challenge I take.

I can change the world
by helping others in need,

with good ideas and my friends,
we'll make a difference indeed.

I can learn from the experts
and those I admire,

with resilience and practice
one day I'll inspire.

So, big or small,
short or tall,

with or without,
the world needs us all.

Let's believe that we can and make a plan,

then celebrate finishing
the things that we began.

Most importantly, always remember,

we may be little, but we can do a lot!

Now It's YOUR Turn

Here are some things that you can do to make a difference

- ❑ Try your best

- ❑ Use good manners

- ❑ Clean up after yourself

- ❑ Give a smile and/or a compliment

- ❑ Pick up trash without being asked

- ❑ Play with someone new during recess

- ❑ Offer help to someone before they ask

- ❑ Help someone who has dropped something

- ❑ Thank an adult for something they do for you

- ❑ Let someone else go first / Hold the door for someone

- ❑ Make a thank you card for a school staff member (principal, custodian, nurse, secretary, playground aide, teacher, etc.)

- ❑ Stand up for someone and/or help someone having a hard day

and with an adult's help, you can try these things:

- ☐ Learn a new skill
- ☐ Make a care package for someone
- ☐ Pull weeds for an elderly neighbor
- ☐ Donate gently used books and/or toys
- ☐ Volunteer for a service project or at a nursing home
- ☐ Make a thank you card for a community helper or veteran
- ☐ Be kind to planet Earth by planting a tree, recycling, or using a reusable water bottle

Write something that you will do to make a difference

☐ _____

_____

"Always remember that you can do a lot."   – Zoe ☺

Words to know

Read the definition, then draw a picture that shows your understanding of the word.

Discipline - To have self-control in training or learning.

Grit - To courageously keep working towards a hard goal.

Persistence - To keep trying and not giving up.

Prevail - To win, succeed or overcome.

Resilience - To bounce back after a failure or a challenge.